Marriage Records for Family Historians

Stuart A. Raymond

VITAL
RECORDS
FOR FAMILY
HISTORIANS
2

THE FAMILY HISTORY PARTNERSHIP

Published by
The Family History Partnership
PO Box 502
Bury, Lancashire BL8 9EP
Webpage: www.familyhistorypartnership.co.uk
Email: sales@thefamilyhistorypartnership.com

in association with
S.A. & M.J. Raymond
Webpage: www.stuartraymond.co.uk
Email: samjraymond@btopenworld.com

ISBNs:
Family History Partnership: 978 1 906280 23 9
S.A. & M.J. Raymond: 978 1 899668 **55 7**

First Published 2010

Printed and bound by
Information Press. Southfield Road, Eynsham
Oxford OX29 4JB

Contents

Acknowledgements

I would like to thank the members of the Family History Partnership for their support, and especially Richard Ratcliffe, who read my manuscript, and Bob Boyd, who saw the book through the press.

1. Introduction

Marriage registers are perhaps the single most important source for tracing family history. A variety of different registers have been kept by parochial incumbents, regimental chaplains, civil registrars, ships masters, and others. The focus of this book is on these registers, and associated documents, as sources for family history. Their strengths and weaknesses will be outlined. General indications of where to find them will be given. The availability of indexes will be discussed. Stress will be placed on using marriage registers and their indexes with a critical eye.

Marriage in church was the norm in England between the end of the medieval period and the late twentieth century. Marriage forms the basis of family life. A wedding marked the beginning of a new household, and perhaps the most important milestone in the history of any family. Weddings were vital events which you must trace if you are going to compile your family tree.

Fortunately, marriages have been recorded for most of the last 500 years, although many early registers have been lost. Centralised civil registration began in 1837, local parish registers in 1538.

When Thomas Cromwell first ordered the clergy to keep parish registers, he had a reasonable expectation that the great majority of marriages would be registered, although he would have realised that a handful that were valid in common law, but not in canon law, would slip through the net. The disconnect between civil and canon law resulted in a rapidly increasing number of 'irregular' marriages until Lord Hardwicke's Marriage Act of 1753 regularised the situation, and abolished common law marriage.

Another problem was created by the growth of nonconformity. From the mid-seventeenth century, the Quakers and other nonconformists conducted their own marriage ceremonies, and kept their own registers. Hardwicke's Act restricted the right to conduct marriage ceremonies to the Church of England, the Quakers, and the Jews. Consequently, marriage registers for most nonconformists ceased after 1753, and were not resumed until 1899.

Hardwicke's Act did not, however, solve all the problems of the registration system. Secularisation and urbanisation in the early nineteenth-century meant that many babies were not baptised. In addition, the number of nonconformist baptisms was growing. These two trends meant that increasing numbers of babies were not recorded in Church of

England baptism registers. Parish registers could therefore no longer be relied upon to prove descent. But the ability to prove descent was vital for the administration of inheritance laws. Parliament, dominated by landowners, felt compelled to act. It legislated in 1836 for the introduction of a new system of civil registration of births, marriages and deaths. The Church of England, however, successfully insisted that the initial registration of marriages should continue to be the responsibility of the parochial clergy. Henceforward, the systems of civil and ecclesiastical registration of marriages duplicated each other. Curiously, only marriage was treated in this way. Baptismal registration by parish clergy also continued, but the ecclesiastical registers were quite separate from the civil birth registers.

Parliament's motivation in introducing civil registration is worth emphasising. The introduction of civil registration was seen as essential for the administration of inheritance laws. Efficiently kept registers were considered to offer the best proof of descent. Civil and parish registers are almost the only sources available to genealogists which were specifically designed for genealogical purposes.

2. Civil Registers

2A. *Introduction*
Every marriage which has taken place in England and Wales since 1st July 1837 should be recorded in the registers compiled for the General Register Office (GRO). If a marriage took place in an Anglican church, a Quaker meeting house, or a Jewish synagogue (or, after 1898, in a registered nonconformist chapel) there should be three copies of every entry. Celebrants were made responsible for compiling the registers, in duplicate, in printed books supplied by District Registrars. One copy was to be retained by the church, the other was to be deposited with the District Registrar on completion. The clergyman also had to send in quarterly returns of entries in the register to the Registrar General. If the marriage took place in the Registry Office, rather than in church, then the District Registrar kept his own register, not in duplicate, and made his returns to the Registrar General.

The original registers are now held by district registrars, local record offices, or in church safes. The duplicates compiled by clergy for return to district registrars may still be in church safes, as they are only deposited when they have been completely filled in - which may take a very long time in small churches. The registers compiled for the church are parish registers. Unless they are still in use, these are likely to have been deposited in local record offices. These are the only registers which are normally open to direct public inspection. If they are still held in church safes, then inspection is at the discretion of clergy or church officers.

The registers held by the GRO are transcripts of the copies sent to the central office by clergy and district registrars. As such, they are open to all the errors which can be made by copyists. The indexes to GRO registers are also liable to error, so much so that two books have been written on the subject.[1] The GRO is currently creating an entirely new index. It is better, if possible, to rely on the original registers. Unfortunately, the registers held by both district registrars and the GRO are not open to direct public inspection. It is necessary to apply for certificates in order to obtain the information they contain. Applications for GRO certificates must cite the information provided in its indexes. For certificates from district registrars, see below.

The GRO's indexes are available on a number of websites, and also on microfilm and microfiche. Locations are given by:

- Holders of the GRO Indexes
  www.direct.gov.uk/dr_consum_dg/groups/dg_digitalassets/@dg/ @en/documents/digitalasset/dg_176534.pdf

Copies are held by many public libraries, Latter Day Saints Family History Centres (see **www.familysearch.org**), and some family history society libraries (see **www.genuki.org.uk/big/Societies.html**). Digital copies are available on a number of internet sites:

- 192.com
  www.192.com/genealogy
- Ancestry
  www.ancestry.co.uk
- BMD Index
  www.bmdindex.co.uk
- Family Relatives
  www.familyrelatives.com
- Find My Past
  www.findmypast.com
- FreeBMD
  www.freebmd.org.uk
- The Genealogist
  www.thegenealogist.co.uk

---

[1] FOSTER, MICHAEL WHITFIELD. *A comedy of errors, or, the marriage records of England and Wales, 1837-1988.* The author, 1998. FOSTER, MICHAEL WHITFIELD. *A comedy of errors, act 2.* The author 2002.

FreeBMD offers a free service, and is therefore the place to begin your search, although transcription has not yet been completed. The other sites charge on either a pay per view or a subscription basis. Most of them also offer a variety of other databases, for example, the census, so it may be worth paying a subscription to use them. The GRO will search the indexes for you (for a fee), or you can pay your own agent.

Family Relatives offers a unique search facility, which may be worth using, especially if you are searching for a common name. Its 'marriage match' enables you to identify possible spouses without having to obtain certificates. It searches for everyone who married in the same quarter in the same district. This narrows the search down considerably.

The indexes provide the basic information needed to apply for certificates from the GRO (but not from district registrars). They were compiled quarterly. Against each person's name is indicated the registration district, together with the volume and page number of the entry in the registry. Several entries may be on the same page, so these details are not unique to the particular entry required. Since 1911, the surnames of both parties are given together in the marriage index.

If you prefer to obtain certificates from district registries, you will need to identify the registration district in which registration took place. They are listed in:

- LANGSTON, BRETT. *A handbook to the registration districts of England and Wales.* B.Langston, 2001.
- Registration Districts in England and Wales (1837-1930)
  www.ukbmd.org.uk/genuki/reg

You will probably also need to identify the place where the marriage took place before you can obtain a certificate. In recent years, an increasing number of registers held by district registrars have been indexed online. These databases are listed at

- UK BMD: Births, Marriages, Deaths and Censuses on the Internet
  www.ukbmd.org.uk
  (click 'Local BMD')

2B. *Information*
Entries in civil marriage registers (and in post-1837 ecclesiastical marriage registers) include the following information:
1. Place of marriage
2. When married
3. Name and surname
4. Age
5. Condition (i.e. marital status)
6. Rank or profession (if any)
7. Residence at the time of marriage

8. Father's name and surname
9. Rank or profession of father
10. Whether by banns, licence, or registrar's certificate
11. Signatures of parties, minister or registrar, and witnesses.

They also give the registration district, sub-district, year of registration, and the number of the entry in the register.

Entries in both civil and ecclesiastical marriage registers post-1837 are normally identical. However, if amendments were subsequently made in parish registers some time after the entry was made, that will not necessarily be reflected in the civil registers. In cases of doubt, it may be worth checking both entries.

2C. *Problems*

The use of civil registration indexes and certificates may give rise to a number of problems. The inaccuracy of indexing has already been discussed. The second point to note is that the spelling of surnames varied considerably. It is a myth that surname spellings have always been constant. They have not. The spelling you use to check the index may not be the same as in the register. Always check for variant spellings if you do not find the entry you are looking for. Amy may be Amey, Black may be Blacke, Smith may be Smyth. The indexer may have mis-understood hand-writing, confusing capitals such as L, S, and T. Fore-names may also be different. Substituting Smith, Lizzie, for Smith, Elizabeth, will place the index entry far away from where you expect to find it.

There are other reasons why names may differ from your expectation. Widows who re-married should have used their first husband's name for registration purposes, not their maiden name. The latter should, however, be recorded, as certificates also show fathers' names. More difficulty may arise in identifying brides who had changed their names previously for other reasons, e.g. adopting their step-father's name. Bridegrooms also sometimes changed their name. For example, John Drury and Ann Collingwood were known to have married at St. Ives (Huntingdonshire) in 1851. The index to the civil marriage register listed Ann Collingwood, but there was no mention of the name 'Drury'. Ann's certificate was therefore ordered, revealing that her husband was named John Drury Parish. It subsequently transpired that he had been baptised as John Drury, the illegitimate son of Mary Parish at Costessey (Norfolk) in 1834. He obviously wanted to shake off his illegitimate status.

Addresses may also cause problems. Full addresses were rarely given in the early registers. Street numbering was not completed until the late nineteenth century. Before that, just the name of the street might be given, or even just the name of the parish.

Addresses may be problematic for other reasons. The law required banns to be read in the parishes where both parties lived. Some couples may have falsely claimed to be living in the same parish, in order to avoid the cost of banns being read in two parishes. Others may have sought to avoid the requirement that at least one party had to be resident in a particular parish for four weeks before marriage could take place in its parish church. Sometimes, one or both parties took up temporary residence in the parish where they wished to marry. Alternatively, they may have given false addresses.

The ages of the parties may also be questionable. Sometimes, true ages may not have been known. There were a variety of dubious reasons why couples sometimes gave false ages. An old man may not have wanted his true age to be known. A minor may have falsified his age to avoid the need to obtain parental consent. Sometimes marriage certificates unhelpfully note 'of full age', or perhaps '21'. The latter should be treated with suspicion; it may be synonymous with 'of full age', rather than indicating an actual age.

The column headed 'rank or occupation' is not always strictly accurate. The information given may be completely false, or may be embellished to give a mis-leading impression of a person's status. An agricultural labourer, for example, may describe himself as a small-holder, or even a farmer. Similar problems to these are also found in parish registers, to which we now turn.

3. Parish Registers

3A. *History*

As already noted, parish registers of baptisms, marriages, and burials date from 1538. However, not many registers survive from the sixteenth century. Those that do are likely to be transcripts compiled in the early seventeenth century, in accordance with injunctions of 1598 and 1604. These required paper registers to be replaced with parchment. The Civil War and Interregnum of the mid-seventeenth century also badly affected the keeping and survival of registers.

There was no regularity in the form of entry in sixteenth and seventeenth century marriage registers. Frequently, the entries for baptisms, marriages, and burials were made together, rather than being separated. The information given in marriage entries could be minimal, for example, just the name of the groom and the date of marriage. More usually, the name of the bride was given. Other information, such as occupations and addresses, were also given occasionally. Entries in the early register of Ottery St Mary (Devon) are particularly full. For example, we learn from the printed register that Nathaniel Russe, 'servant unto Leonard Olde', and Christian Norrington, the daughter of Johan Norrington, widow, were married on 13th November 1609.

Unusual circumstances sometimes attracted attention. For example, the register of St. James, Bury St. Edmunds, records a marriage that took place on November 5th, 1832: 'Christopher Newsam married Charity Morrell. Charity Morrell being entirely without arms, the ring was placed upon the fourth toe of the left foot, and she wrote her name in this register with her right foot'.

Greater regularity was introduced by Hardwicke's Marriage Act, 1753. Printed forms began to be used for marriage entries, with effect from 1st April 1754. These continued to be used until the introduction of civil registration in 1837. They give the names and parish(es) of the parties, the date and place of marriage, whether by banns or licence, whether with the consent of parents or guardians, the name of the officiating minister, and the signatures of the parties, witnesses, and minister.

3B. *Parish Register Transcripts and Indexes*
Numerous original parish registers have been transcribed and indexed. The differences between an original register, a transcript, and an index are important. Unfortunately, these terms are frequently mis-used by people who should know better - especially web-masters. Transcripts should be exact copies of original registers, letter by letter, word by word. Indexes are alphabetical lists of names in registers, showing where they appear, but not necessarily giving any detail. They are intended to tell you where to look in original registers, not to be substitutes for them. It is the information in original registers that researchers need.

It is very difficult to achieve 100% accuracy in transcripts and indexes. If a name does not appear in them, that is no evidence that it is not in the original register. If possible, it is always desirable to check information from transcripts and indexes against original registers. Indexes in particular are not intended to record everything that is in the original. And even the original may be flawed by scribal incompetence or deliberate falsification.

Original parish registers have usually been deposited in local record offices. Their websites (listed at **www.nationalarchives.gov.uk/archon**) frequently list the registers available. A summary national listing is provided in Cecil Humphery-Smith's *Phillimore atlas and index of parish registers* (3rd ed. Phillimore, 2003). Comprehensive listings of original registers, bishops' transcripts, and other copies, are provided in the county volumes of the *National index of parish registers,* published by the Society of Genealogists. Libraries hold many transcripts of parish registers. Many transcribers make three copies - for the Society of Genealogists, the local studies library, and the local family history society.

Numerous transcripts and indexes of parish registers are available online. They are listed in Stuart Raymond's *Births marriages and deaths on the web* (2nd ed. 2 vols., 2005). Websites mostly provide transcripts or indexes, rather than the digitised images which are really needed. The only substantial collections of digitised images currently available are at Medway Archives **cityark.medway.gov.uk** (click 'parish registers online'), and at 'London Parish Records from 1538' **http:// landing. ancestry.co.uk/lma**. The 'Cheshire Parish Register Project' **www.csc. liv.ac.uk/~cprdb** is currently preparing computerised transcripts of registers for the whole county.

Many parish registers have been published, and are available in libraries world-wide. Over 1400 marriage registers are included in the *Phillimore parish registers* series. Over 100 registers were published by the Parish Register Society. Many counties have had their own parish register societies, including Buckinghamshire, Lancashire **www.lprs.org.uk**, Northumberland and Durham, Shropshire, Staffordshire **www.sprs. org.uk**, Surrey, and Yorkshire **www.yorkshireparishregisters.com**. Many registers for London and other counties were published by the Harleian Society **http://fmg.ac/Harleian**. Bedfordshire County Council **www.bedfordshire.gov.uk** has published all of the county's pre-1812 registers. The Parish Register Transcription Society **www.prtsoc.org.uk** has recently commenced publishing registers for Hampshire, Norfolk, West Sussex, and elsewhere. Some county record societies, for example, those for Devon and Cornwall and for Cumberland and Westmorland have issued many registers for their areas. Family history societies have also published many registers. These are usually listed on the publications pages of society websites (gatewayed at **www.genuki.org.uk/ Societies**). Many published registers, especially from the Phillimore series, can be found in digitised format on web pages.

3C. *Further Information*

A much more detailed guide to parish registers than can be given here is provided by:
- RAYMOND, STUART A. *Parish registers: a history and guide.* Family History Partnership, 2009.

4. Associated Records

4A. *Bishops Transcripts (BTs)*

These are the returns of parish register entries made annually by the parochial clergy to bishops. They date from the sixteenth century until the introduction of civil registration, sometimes later. They can be particularly useful where original registers have been lost. At Falmouth, for example, there are no marriage entries in the original registers between

1672 and 1698. Details can, however, be supplied from BTs for late 1672, 1678, 1683, 1685, and 1697. Unfortunately, there are no BTs for the other missing years.

The survival of BTs generally is patchy. They were usually written on loose sheets of paper which could easily be lost. None were made during the Interregnum (1649-60). Many 'peculiars', that is, areas outside of the normal jurisdiction of a bishop, did not send them in at all until an act of 1812 required them to do so. Bishops transcripts can be found amongst diocesan records in local record offices, and are listed by Gibson (see below).

BTs and marriage registers should always be compared with each other. In theory, they should be identical. In practice, some BTs abbreviate entries in the parish register, but others may provide more information. That additional information could be useful.

4B. *Banns*

Banns are notices of intended marriages proclaimed in public. They were rarely recorded prior to Hardwicke's Marriage Act 1753. Since then, they have been recorded in printed books, sometimes in the same book that was used for the marriage register, although this practice ceased in 1837. Many banns registers have been lost. Nevertheless, it is worth checking whether they do survive. If the parties lived in different parishes, there should be entries in two separate registers. Comparison of both entries with the marriage register may provide additional information about the couple.

An entry in a banns register does not prove that the proposed marriage actually took place. Indeed, sometimes it is stated that the marriage did not take place. The banns of Joseph Nash, bachelor, and Anne Hare, widow, are recorded in the banns register of Heckington, Lincolnshire, on 31st July, 1836. A note indicates that they were withdrawn; the bride to be instead married the father of Joseph Nash! The fact of marriage can usually only be proved by an entry in a marriage register.

4C. *Marriage Licence Records*

The need for banns to be called could be circumvented by obtaining a marriage licence. Licences avoided the need to wait for three weeks before the ceremony could take place. They were necessary if a couple wanted to marry away from home. They were preferred by nonconformists, who wanted as little to do with the Church of England as possible, and by the gentry, who thought it vulgar to have banns called in church. Licences could be granted by bishops, archbishops, some archdeacons, and their surrogates.

Actual licences rarely survive; they were given to the couple, who presented it to the officiating clergyman as proof of their entitlement to marry. However, registers of licences granted were sometimes kept, as were the documents used to apply for them. The Society of Genealogists does have a collection of original marriage licences presented to officiants in London. These are described in:

- CHURCHILL, ELSE. '*Munimenta antiqua* and Crisp's and Clench's collections of original apprenticeship indentures 1641-1888, and original marriage licences', *Genealogists' magazine* **28**(3), 2004, p.101-3.

The first stage in applying for a marriage licence was to submit an allegation. Allegations usually give names, ages, places of abode, and occupations/status of both spouses. If a minor was involved, the name of a consenting parent should also have been given.

Between 1579 and 1823, a marriage bond was also required. This was intended to give security to the issuers if certain conditions were not met. There had to be no impediment to the marriage, parental consent had to have been given if necessary, and - from 1604 - the marriage had to take place in a parish where one of the parties lived. The two witnesses who were bound - usually including the groom - stood to lose the amount specified in the bond if these conditions were not met. The first part of the bond was in Latin, but this should not deter researchers. The Latin is common form, and not particularly relevant. The useful information that bonds provide are the names of both the couple and the witnesses, the date of the bond, and sometimes addresses and occupations.

Like entries in banns registers, the existence of a marriage allegation or a bond does not prove that a marriage actually took place. The proof needed is usually an entry in a marriage register.

Marriage bonds and allegations can usually be found amongst the diocesan archives in local record offices. Most have been indexed; many have been printed, although not always accurately. It is worth checking for both a bond and an allegation; they may provide different information.

4D. *Further Information*

Bishops transcripts, banns registers, and marriage licence records, all survive amongst diocesan records in local record offices. Details of the availability of bishops' transcripts and marriage licence records is given in:

- GIBSON, JEREMY. *Bishops' transcripts and marriage licences ...* 4th ed. FFHS, 1997.

The county volumes of the *National index of parish registers* provide detailed listings of bishops transcripts and banns registers for each parish. This information may also sometimes be found on Genuki **www.genuki.org.uk** parish pages.

5. Nonparochial Registers

Marriages conducted by clergymen of the Church of England were not necessarily conducted in parish churches. A variety of other institutions, for example, hospitals and schools, had chapels where marriages could be conducted in accordance with the rites of the Church of England. Their records are listed in the county volumes of the *National index of parish registers*. Some of these non-parochial registers have been deposited in the National Archives (TNA), for example, registers of London's Foundling Hospital, and of Greenwich Hospital. These are being made available at BMD Registers **www.bmdregisters.org.uk**.

TNA also holds a collection of late nineteenth- and early twentieth-century registers from Army garrison chapels in the UK. These have recently been deposited by the Royal Army Chaplains Department, and are listed by

- McGOWAN, ALAN. 'Garrison church registers', *Genealogists' magazine* **29**(9), 2009, p.341-2.

6. Irregular Marriages

Irregular marriages (sometimes referred to as 'clandestine') were usually marriages that were conducted without the calling of banns or the granting of licences. Until 1753, such marriages were valid in common law, but not in canon law. Bishops could prosecute priests who conducted irregular marriages, but they could not invalidate the marriages. The origin of this disconnect between common and canon law lay in the medieval period. Marriage had originally been simply an agreement made by the parties in front of witnesses. Gradually, the custom of obtaining a blessing from the church developed; by the sixteenth century this custom was universal - but it was not binding in common law. And betrothals made before a church ceremony was conducted were popularly regarded as marriage.

There were many liberties and peculiars in England which were outside of the jurisdiction of bishops. Some of these places became centers where marriages could be conducted cheaply, without banns or licences, and in private. They were popular. In the late seventeenth century, the ecclesiastical authorities fought running battles against such marriage centres. Legislation in 1695 stamped out the trade at places such as St. Botolph's, Aldgate and Holy Trinity, Minories. However, the legislation merely diverted the trade to other venues, especially the Fleet Prison. This was a royal peculiar, outside the Bishop of London's jurisdiction. It was a debtor's prison - and some of the debtors were clergymen, who had nothing to fear from episcopal censure. In the years immediately prior to 1753, it has been estimated that up to a half of London's marriages were conducted there. Hardwicke's Marriage Act 1753 made irregular marriages invalid, and put a stop to them. The history of irregular marriages is outlined in:

- BENTON, TONY. *Irregular marriages in London before 1754.* 2nd ed. Society of Genealogists, 2000.

Fleet celebrants kept their own registers, many of which are now in TNA class RG 7. See:

- Fleet Registers
  **www.nationalarchives.gov.uk/catalogue/
  rdleaflet.asp?sLeafletID=417**

Some Fleet registers have been published:

- HERBER, MARK, ed. *Clandestine marriages in the Chapel and Rules of the Fleet Prison, 1680-1754.* 3 vols to date. Francis Boutle Publishers, 1998-2001.

Fleet marriages have been digitised and made available on the internet at 'BMD Registers' **www.bmdregisters.org.uk**. A few Fleet registers are indexed by the *IGI* (see below, p.23). In view of their irregular and unofficial nature, these registers need to be used with care.

Hardwicke's Act put a stop to irregular marriages in England and Wales. It did not, however, apply outside of England and Wales. Many couples eloped to Scotland, or to the Channel Islands, in order to take advantage of less rigourous marriage laws. Details of available Scottish registers are given in 'Irregular Border and Scottish Runaway Marriages' **www.gro-scotland.gov.uk/files1/family-records/irregular-border-and-scottish-runaway-marriages.pdf**. Over 4,500 marriages are recorded in Achievements' Gretna Green Index **www.achievements.co.uk/services/gretna/index.php**, which covers 1795-1895. The register from which this index is taken should, like the Fleet registers, be used with care.

7. Nonconformist Registers

Since 1898, nonconformist marriage registers have been duplicates of the civil registers. If register books have been completely filled in, the District Registrar will have one copy. The copy that was intended to be retained by the church will probably be in a local record office, unless it is still in use. Marriage certificates can be obtained from both the GRO and district registrars, as outlined above.

Between 1837 and 1898, most marriages in nonconformist chapels were registered by district registrars. Congregations kept no separate records. Between 1753 and 1837, nonconformist marriages had to take place in the Church of England. Consequently, there are rarely separate registers. The only exception to this rule were the Quakers, who were allowed to marry in their own meeting houses. Their registers are discussed below.

Between 1660 and 1752, nonconformists sometimes kept their own marriage registers. These sometimes covered large areas, or were used by a number of different churches. Nonconformist registers were sometimes regarded as the property of the minister, rather than belonging to the church. The same register therefore may record events in widely separated churches where the same pastor had ministered. For example, the Kings Lynn Presbyterian church register for 1754 to 1777 is in the same volume as entries from Maidenhead for 1745 to 1749.

There was no set form of entry in most nonconformist registers (apart from the Quakers). One suspects that some were written up from memory or scraps of paper long after marriages took place. This can be deduced from entries such as the following from the Northowram register in 1704: 'Mr. John Taylor Minr in the Dales, and Mrs Elizabeth Ellet, married abt Midsummer'. The celebrant obviously could not remember the exact date.

Not many nonconformist registers survive. Many of those which do were surrendered to the Registrar General after the introduction of civil registration, and are now in TNA, class RG 4 and RG 8. Two attempts to create nation-wide registers of dissenters are now in RG 5. These are the Protestant Dissenters Register, 1743-1837, and the Wesleyan Metropolitan Registry, 1818-38. All of these registers are now available online at:

- BMD Registers
  www.bmdregisters.co.uk

Other registers have been deposited in local record offices and elsewhere. All surviving nonconformist registers, with their locations, are listed in the county volumes of the *National index of parish registers*. Lists of registers for each denomination are included in another series of books published by the Society of Genealogists:

- BREED, GEOFFREY. *My ancestors were Baptists: how can I find out more about them?* 4th ed. Society of Genealogists, 2007.
- CLIFFORD, DAVID J.H. *My ancestors were Congregationalists in England and Wales: how can I find out more about them?* 2nd ed. Society of Genealogists, 1997.
- RUSTON, ALAN. *My ancestors were English Presbyterians or Unitarians: how can I find out more about them?* 2nd ed. Society of Genealogists Enterprises, 2001.

- LEARY, WILLIAM. *My ancestors were Methodists: how can I find out more about them?* *4th* ed. Society of Genealogists Enterprises, 2005.

The standard guide to nonconformist registers is still:
- STEEL, D.J. *Sources for nonconformist genealogy and family history*. National index of parish registers **2**. Society of Genealogists, 1973.

8. Quaker Registers

The Quakers were renowned for the quality of their registers, and Hardwicke's Act of 1753 exempted them from the requirement to marry in the Church of England. They had their own dating system, which involved numbering the days and months, rather than using the usual (pagan) names. Most pre-1837 Quaker registers are held by TNA, class RG 6, and are available on **www.bmdregisters.co.uk**. A full listing is provided by:
- *General Register Office. Society of Friends registers, notes, and certificates of births, marriages and deaths.* List & Index Society **267**. 1996.

Before their registers were deposited, Quakers compiled digests of the information in them. These digests record some 40,000 marriages, and are now held by Friends House Library **www.quaker.org.uk/ library**. They have been published on microfilm; the reels are available in a number of major research libraries. See:
- *Quaker digest registers of births, marriages and burials for England and Wales, c.1650-1837.* 32 reels + pamphlet. World Microfilms Publications, 1989.

These digests do not necessarily include all the information given in the original registers. The latter should therefore be consulted if an entry is found in the digests.

Quakers had to obtain the permission of their Meetings to marry. Preparative and Monthly Meeting minutes record much information about the investigations undertaken when members applied for permission. These minutes can usually be found in local record offices. If an ancestor was a Quaker, it would be well worth while to check them, as they may give much more information than the mere register entry. Detailed information about Quaker records is given in:
- MILLIGAN, EDWARD H., & THOMAS, MALCOLM J. *My ancestors were Quakers: how can I find out more about them?* 2nd ed. Society of Genealogists, 1999.

See also:
- MILLIGAN, EDWARD. *Quaker marriage*. Quaker Tapestry Scheme, 1994.

9. Huguenot Registers

The Huguenots were refugees from France and the Low Countries, who formed their own churches in England in the late sixteenth and seventeenth centuries. Some of them accepted supervision from English bishops, others did not. Huguenot registers are usually in French. In the printed register of the Canterbury Huguenots, we read of the marriage of 'Francois Guilleman, fils de Nicolas, natif de St. Aubin, et Anne De la Mer, fille de Jacob, natifue de Canterbory' on 3rd January 1657-8.

The Canterbury register is accompanied by a collection of 'marriage contracts', which provide valuable information about the 'assistants' of the bride and groom. The contract for Francois and Nicolas, for example, names his uncle and cousin, and her father, uncles, and brother-in-law, together with a number of witnesses.

Huguenot registers were generally deposited with the Registrar General in 1841, and are now in TNA, class RG 4. All deposited registers have been published, mostly by the Huguenot Society **www.huguenot society.org.uk.** These publications can be consulted in many libraries. The original registers are currently being digitised at **www.bmd registers. co.uk**.

10. Roman Catholic Registers

Roman Catholicism was the official religion of England until Henry VIII broke with Rome in 1534. Parish registers for the reign of Mary, 1553-8, are Roman Catholic records. After 1558, Roman Catholics became a persecuted minority. Consequently, they kept few marriage registers in the first two centuries after the Reformation. If Roman Catholics could not prove the legitimacy of their marriage, they were liable to be presented for 'fornication'. Records of such presentations can sometimes be found amongst the archives of church courts.[2] These archives may contain the only record of such marriages.

Until 1753, Roman Catholic marriages were legal if they could be proved. Hardwicke's Marriage Act of that year removed legal recognition from marriages conducted by Roman Catholic priests. Catholics therefore frequently went through two ceremonies: an Anglican service to satisfy the law of the land, and a Catholic service to satisfy conscience. Roman Catholic marriage registers gradually became more common in the late eighteenth and early nineteenth centuries. Marriages were frequently registered twice - in the Anglican parish register, and in the Roman Catholic marriage register. Roman Catholic registers may pro-

---

[2] For church court records, consult Tarver, Anne. *Church court records: an introduction for family and local historians.* Phillimore, 1995.

vide more information than the parish register. They may even indicate the parish in which the legal service was conducted.

After 1837, most Roman Catholic churches were licenced for marriages to be conducted in the presence of a registrar, who entered details in the civil registers. Some priests kept their own separate registers. The register for Newport, Isle of Wight, was kept in Latin, even in the middle of the nineteenth century. It usually recorded 'nullo legitime impedimento detecto' in each marriage entry, and gave the names of all parents, with their residences.

From 1898, Roman Catholic priests were able to record the marriages they conducted in the civil registers, in the dual system already discussed.

Roman Catholics had the opportunity to deposit their records with the Registrar General in 1841, but few did so. Those which were deposited are now in TNA, and are available at BMD Registers **www.bmdregisters.org.uk**. Many others have been deposited in local record offices. A full listing, with locations, is published in:

- GANDY, MICHAEL. *Catholic missions and registers*. 6 vols + atlas vol. The author, 1993.

A number of Catholic marriage registers have been published by the Catholic Record Society **www.catholic-history.org.uk/crs/records.htm**. These are available in many libraries. The standard guide to Roman Catholic registers is:

- STEEL, D.J., & SAMUEL, EDGAR R. *Sources for Roman Catholic and Jewish genealogy and family history*. National index of parish registers **3**. Phillimore, for the Society of Genealogists, 1974.

11. Jewish Registers

Before the introduction of civil registration in 1837, there were no legal provisions governing Jewish marriage procedures and registration. Jews were exempted from the provisions of Hardwicke's Marriage Act 1753. Since 1837, Jewish marriage registers have been compiled in duplicate, with one copy for the district registrar, in the dual system of civil registration already described. Provision is made in the Jewish registers for the address at which a marriage takes place to be recorded, as they could be conducted anywhere, not necessarily in synagogues.

A Jewish marriage requires two witness. It also requires the bride to be given a marriage contract, or ketubah. Copies of ketubot issued from the mid-nineteenth century onwards can be found amongst synagogue archives. These are generally still held by Synagogue officers. Ketubot from one important synagogue have been published:

- *Abstracts of the Ketubot or marriage-contracts and of the civil marriage registers of the Spanish and Portuguese Jews' Congregation for the period 1837- 1901*. Spanish and Portuguese Jews' Congregation / Jewish Historical Society of England, 1973.

From c.1845 onwards, the United Synagogue required parties to obtain a marriage authorisation certificate. These authorized local rabbis to conduct the marriage. A database of these certificates is currently being compiled:

- Marriage Authorisation Certificate Records
  www.theus.org.uk/support_services/find_your_family/
  marriage_records

Details of English synagogues and their records, including a number of marriage databases, can be found at:
- JCR-UK: Jewish Communities and Records: United Kingdom
  www.jewishgen.org/jcr-uk

There are two important textbooks:
- JOSEPH, ANTHONY. *My ancestors were Jewish*. 4th ed. Society of Genealogists Enterprises, 2008.
- STEEL, D.J., & SAMUEL, EDGAR R. *Sources for Roman Catholic and Jewish genealogy and family history*. National index of parish registers **3**. Phillimore, for the Society of genealogists, 1974.

See also:
- Tips for Finding Marriage Documents from Jewish Marriages in England
  www.jgsgb.org.uk/engmarr.shtml

12. Overseas Registers
Overseas marriages had to be conducted in accordance with the marriage laws of the countries where they took place, and it may be necessary to consult the local civil and parish registers to trace them.
A gateway to overseas websites is provided by:
- Cyndis List: Marriages
  www.cyndislist.com/marriage.htm

Registers relating to marriages that took place in British consulates and embassies, overseas Anglican churches and chaplaincies, the armed forces, and on board ship, are available in Britain, in a number of repositories. Many are held by TNA. Some of these duplicate registers in the GRO, and in the Guildhall Library.

Registers of marriages at sea were kept by masters of merchant ships, and deposited with the Registrar General of Shipping and Seamen. The original registers are now in TNA, class BT 158 for 1854-90; class BT 334/117 for 1854-1972. Some of the early entries in BT334/117 duplicate entries in BT 158. Entries in both these classes should have been certified to the GRO, but it is likely that many do not appear in the GRO's registers. Databases of BT 158 are available on two websites, FindMyPast **www.findmypast.com** (from 1854-83) and BMD Registers **www.bmd registers.co.uk** (for 1854-1908).

TNA has a few registers of marriages aboard ships of the Royal Navy, 1842-89 (RG 33/156, indexed in RG 43/7), together with a variety of non-statutory records deposited by the Registrar General. These include (in RG 32) many certificates issued by overseas registration authorities, documents sent in by individuals, and copies of entries made in registers by overseas Anglican incumbents and chaplains. Similar collections are in RG 33 and RG 34. RG 36 consists of returns made by civil registration officers in some British colonies. Indexes of these series are in RG 43.

Marriage registers can also be found amongst Foreign Office records, in various TNA classes. These relate to marriages conducted in overseas consulates. The Foreign Office conducted extensive correspondence relating to marriages abroad. 46 volumes of correspondence, covering the period 1814-1905, can be found in FO 83 and FO 97. There is an index in FO 802/239 covering 1814-93. Information on individual marriages is included.

A full list of registers held by TNA can be found in:
* BEVAN, AMANDA. *Tracing your ancestors in the National Archives: the Website and beyond.* 7th ed. The National Archives, 2006.

The General Register Office holds registers of marriages at sea from 1837. These are compiled from information provided by the Registrar General of Shipping and Seamen, as discussed above. They cannot be consulted directly. An application for a marriage certificate must by made to the GRO **www.direct.gov.uk/en/Governmentcitizensand rights/Registeringlifeevents/Familyhistoryandresearch/index.htm**. This also applies to the variety of consular and armed forces registers they hold. Statutory (but not compulsory) registration of the marriages of British citizens overseas began in 1849, although a few earlier consular registers are held. Regimental and chaplains' registers commence in 1761. Microfilm of these registers are held by TNA, who also hold indexes in RG 43.

Many registers of overseas Anglican chaplaincies can be found amongst the records of the Diocese of London and the Diocese of Gibraltar. Most of these begin in the eighteenth or nineteenth centuries. Between 1816 and 1924, the Bishop of London's registry maintained a series of volumes of *International memoranda* for the registration of overseas vital events. The certificates sent in by overseas clergy were also retained. All of these records are now held in Guildhall Library. For details, see:

- Births, Marriages and Deaths Overseas
  www.history.ac.uk/gh/overseas.htm

Another important collection of registers is held by the British Library, in its India Office collections. The chaplains of the East India Company regularly sent returns of all baptisms, marriages and burials to London. These returns do not just cover the Indian sub-continent; they cover all the Company's possessions, from St. Helena in the Atlantic to Macao in China. A full description is given by:

- Ecclesiastical Records
  **www.bl.uk/reshelp/findhelpregion/asia/ india/
      indiaofficerecordsfamilyhistory/ecclesiastical/eccrecords.html**

The returns can be inspected in the British Library, but are also available on an internet database:

- India Family History Search
  http://indiafamily.bl.uk/UI/Home.aspx

A detailed guide to registers of vital events at sea is provided by:

- WATTS, CHRISTOPHER T., & WATTS, MICHAEL J. *Tracing births, deaths, and marriages at sea.* Society of Genealogists Enterprises, 2004.

For overseas registers, consult:

- YEO, GEOFFREY. *The British Overseas: a guide to records of their births, baptisms, marriages, deaths and burials available in the United Kingdom.* 3rd ed, Guildhall Library, 1994.

A more general guide to overseas research is provided by:

- KERSHAW, ROGER. *Emigrants and expats: a guide to sources on UK emigration and residents overseas.* Public Record Office, 2002.

13. Marriage Indexes

Numerous indexes to marriage registers have been compiled. Some of these, including the GRO index to civil registers, have already been mentioned. These indexes can be very useful. However, it remains true that a very substantial proportion of marriage entries in parish registers are not covered in the indexes discussed below. Coverage is far from complete.

Indexes, it must be remembered, are only indexes - they index the original registers, or perhaps transcripts of those registers, but they do not necessarily reproduce the information in them. Their function is to tell you where to look. It is then up to you to check the sources they identify. Don't assume that they provide all the information available. The *IGI*, for example, does not include the names of witnesses which can be found in post-1754 registers.

The *IGI* (or, to give it its full title, the *International Genealogical Index*), is the single most important index to marriage registers. This is an on-going project run by the Church of Jesus Christ of Latter Day Saints (LDS), popularly known as the Mormons. It is available online at Family Search **www.familysearch.org**. Many libraries hold a fiche version, which was issued in 1992. The *IGI* is also available on CD as the *British vital records index* (2nd ed. 2002). This can be purchased via 'Family Search'. Indexing is still in progress, so it is best to use the website, as it is more up to date. It also provides more information than either the microfiche or the CD. The documents it indexes have been microfilmed by the Family History Library in Salt Lake City.

There are two sources for entries in the *IGI*. 'Extracted records' include marriage registers from all denominations, as well as overseas registers. 'Submitted records' have been submitted by researchers tracing their own families, and can sometimes be very questionable. 'Extracted records' should also be treated with a degree of caution. There will always be errors in indexes.

The *IGI* entry gives you a microfilm batch number which can be used to borrow a copy of the document indexed, through the world-wide network of LDS Family History Centres. It is quite likely to provide more information than the index entry. Alternatively (and preferably) you could use the *IGI* information to find the entry in the original register.

Registers filmed and indexed by the *IGI* are listed on Hugh Wallis's 'IGI Batch Numbers' site **freepages.genealogy.rootsweb.ancestry.com/~hughwallis/IGIBatchNumbers.htm**. 'Genuki' parish pages **www.genuki.org.uk** also frequently provide film numbers of local registers that have been copied.

The documents microfilmed and indexed by the *LDS* are not necessarily original parish registers. They may be, but, equally, many bishops transcripts, published registers, and other copies, have been microfilmed. It is important to know the status of the document you are examining.

There are a wide variety of other indexes. The largest is probably Boyd's Index, compiled between 1925 and 1955. The original index is held by the Society of Genealogists and a number of other repositories. It is now available online at 'British Origins' **www.britishorigins.com**, on a pay per view basis. Boyd's is primarily based on copies (not originals) of parish registers, bishops' transcripts, marriage licences, and a few banns registers. Some 7,000,000 names from 4300 registers are indexed - perhaps 15% of all English marriages between 1538 and 1837. The index is nation-wide in its scope.

Pallot's index, now held by the Institute of Heraldic & Genealogical Studies, in Canterbury **http://www.ihgs.ac.uk/index.html**, is also substantial, and nation-wide in its scope, but with a particular strength in the City of London. Most entries date from the late eighteenth and early nineteenth centuries. A database is available on Ancestry **www.ancestry.co.uk** This index is also available on CD.

There are over 1,000,000 entries in the 'Joiner Marriage Index' **www.joinermarriageindex.com**, which offers a pay per view service. Coverage extends from Northumberland to Buckinghamshire.

Many small marriage indexes compiled by family history societies are available at 'Find My Past' **www.findmypast.org.uk**. These were originally available at Family History Online **www.familyhistory online. org.uk.** Not all the indexes on this site were transferred to FindMy Past, and the original website should be consulted for indexes that may now be available elsewhere.

Many other marriage indexes are listed by:
* Gibson, Jeremy, Hampson, Elizabeth, & Raymond, Stuart. *Marriage indexes for family historians*. 9th ed. Family History Partnership, 2008.

14. Channel Islands
Each of the islands has a different system of civil registration. Dates of civil marriage registers are as follows:
* Alderney from 1886, with some gaps.
* Jersey from 1842
* Guernsey from 1919
* Sark from 1925

Addresses of registrars are as follows:
Alderney: The Greffier, Registry for Births, Deaths, Companies, Land and Marriages, St Anne, Alderney GY9 3AA
Guernsey: H.M. Greffier, The Royal Court House, St Peter Port, Guernsey GY1 2PB
Jersey: The Superintendent Registrar, 10 Royal Square, St. Helier, Jersey JE2 4WA
Sark: The Greffe, La Chasse Marette, Sark GY9 0SF

Many parish registers are still with incumbents, although some have been deposited. A full list, with locations, is given in:

- WEBB, CLIFF. *National index of parish registers … Channel Islands and the Isle of Man.* Society of Genealogists, 2000.

The Channel Islands Family History Society **www.channelislands history.com** has transcribed and indexed most Jersey registers. Many microfilms of Guernsey registers are available in the Priaulx Library. The library also holds copies of the civil registers 1840-2004, with indexes. Visit:
- Priaulx Library
  www.priaulxlibrary.co.uk/priaulx-library-collections-genealogy.asp

Many original parish and civil registers for Jersey are held by:
- Société Jersiaise
  www.societe-jersiaise.org/library

15. Ireland

The administration of civil registration in Ireland is similar to its administration in England and Wales. Marriage certificates are almost identical. However, protestant marriages in Ireland have only been registered since 1st April 1845. Roman Catholic marriage registration began on 1st January 1864. From 1st January 1922 vital events in Northern Ireland have been registered separately. Indexes to civil registers are not available online, although they have been computerised. The websites of the two General Register Offices (which include lists of district registrars) are as follows:
- General Register Office [Eire]
  www.groireland.ie
- General Register Office (Northern Ireland)
  www.groni.gov.uk

District registrars are also listed by
- Superintendant Registrars Districts by County
  www.rootsweb.ancestry.com/~bifhsusa/irishregnc.html

Copies of most civil registration indexes are held by the LDS Family History Library, and are available through its network of Family History Centres. They also hold copies of the actual registers for some years. Some civil registration entries can be found in the *IGI*.

Indexes up to 1877 were annual; thereafter they were quarterly. They include the basic information needed to order certificates, that is, the name, the Registration District, and the volume and page number in which the entry is recorded. These indexes cannot be used with the registers held by district registrars. Indexes to these are quite separate, sometimes held by Irish Family History Foundation Centres **www.irish-roots.ie**.

More information is provided by a number of webpages:
- Family Search Research Wiki: Ireland Church Records
  wiki.familysearch.org/en/Ireland_Church_Records
- National Archives of Ireland: Parish Registers and Marriage Licences
  www.nationalarchives.ie/genealogy/church.html
- Civil Registration
  freepages.genealogy.rootsweb.ancestry.com/
  ~irishancestors/Civil%20registration.html
- Ireland Research Outline: Civil Registration
  www.familysearch.org
  Click 'Research Helps', 'Articles', 'I', and title
- A Guide to the General Register Office of Ireland
  homepage.eircom.net/%257Eseanjmurphy/gro

Irish ecclesiastical marriage registers are also available. There are, however, three major differences from English registers. Firstly, more than half of the registers of the Church of Ireland were destroyed by fire in 1922, together with most bishops' transcripts. Secondly, the Church of Ireland, although it was the established church, was not the dominant church. Most Irish were Roman Catholics. There were also many Presbyterians (especially in Northern Ireland), and a number of other denominations. Researchers should note that Roman Catholic and Church of Ireland parishes do not necessarily have the same boundaries or the same names. Thirdly, few marriage registers of any denomination pre-date the late eighteenth century. Irish politics have seldom been conducive to good record keeping.

Many registers of all denominations have been microfilmed for the LDS Family History Library, and indexed in the *IGI* (see above, p.22-3) The Public Record of Northern Ireland also holds many microfilms of registers from all denominations. For these, see:
- Family History: Key Source
  www.proni.gov.uk/index/family_history/
  family_history_key_sources.htm

Most surviving Church of Ireland registers for the Irish Republic (a few of which have been published) are now deposited in the
- Representative Church Body Library
  www.library.ireland.anglican.org

Roman Catholic registers are mostly in local custody. However, almost all pre-1880 registers have been microfilmed. For a list, see:
- National Library of Ireland: Parish Registers
  www.nli.ie/en/parish-register.aspx

A comprehensive listing of register transcripts and indexes *etc* is provided by:
- Irish Ancestors Roman Catholic records
  www.irishtimes.com/ancestor/browse/counties/rcmaps

Presbyterian registers are mostly still in local custody. Some registers are held by:
- Presbyterian Historical Society of Ireland
  www.presbyterianhistoryireland.com/index.php?id=library

Most Methodist registers are still in church custody. The Public Record Office of Northern Ireland has many microfilms for churches in the Province.

Quaker registers are held in the Dublin Friends Historical Library, and by the Society of Friends Ulster Quarterly Meeting. For contact details, visit **www.quakers-in-ireland.ie.** Many Northern Ireland Quaker registers are available on microfilm at the Public Record Office of Northern Ireland.

A comprehensive guide to Irish ecclesiastical registers is provided by:
- RYAN, JAMES G., ed. *Irish Church Records.* Glenageary, County Dublin, Ireland: Flyleaf Press, 1992.

Numerous webpages are devoted to Irish marriage registers. These are listed in:
- RAYMOND, STUART A. *Irish family history on the web: a directory.* 3rd ed. Family History Partnership, 2007.

16. Isle of Man

Voluntary civil registration of marriages in the Isle of Man commenced in 1849, but it did not become compulsory until 1878. The records are at the General Registry, Finch Road, Douglas, Isle of Man. A detailed listing of Manx registers is provided in:
- WEBB, CLIFF. *National index of parish registers … Channel Island and the Isle of Man.* Society of Genealogists, 2000.

Another list, with many extracts, can be viewed at:
- A Manx Note Book: Genealogy
  www.isle-of-man.com/manxnotebook/famhist/genealgy/index.htm

17. Scotland

Family history research in Scotland is far easier than it is in Ireland, or, indeed, in England. This is due to one website:

- Scotlands People
  www.scotlandspeople.gov.uk

This website has databases of both the civil registers and the old parish registers, as well as the census, probate records, and other sources. Civil registration in Scotland began on 1st January 1855. Marriage registers give full name, age, marital status, occupation, usual residence, date and place of marriage (giving religious denomination), name and occupation of father, name and maiden name of mother, and names of witnesses and the officiating clergy. They also include birth places, numbers of former marriages, and the number of children by those marriages. Birth places and previous marriage details were dropped after the first year, but birth places were restored from 1972. Scotlands People's database currently includes digitised images of both the original paper indexes 1855-2006, and the actual registers, 1855-1934.

The site also has indexes to overseas consular returns of marriages from 1917, the Register of Marriages in Foreign Countries for 1860-1965, and Service Returns, 1881-1959, covering army personnel. Currently, images of these records are only available up to 1933.

For civil registers not yet available on Scotlands People, it may be necessary to pay a personal visit to
- Scotlands People Centre
  www.scotlandspeoplehub.gov.uk

The Centre has computerized indexes to all civil registers, to the old parish registers, and to a variety of overseas registers. If you are not able to visit, then application can be made for certificates direct to:
- General Register Office for Scotland
  www.gro-scotland.gov.uk

Microfilm copies of Scottish civil register indexes, 1955-1920 are also held by the LDS Family History Library, and by the Society of Genealogists. The old parish registers were compiled by incumbents of the established (Presbyterian) Church of Scotland. A few commence in 1553, but most are much later. There was no set format, and no equivalent to English bishops' transcripts. Unlike parish registers in England, Scottish registers are all in the same place. They have been deposited with the Scottish Registrar General. Scotlands People provides a full index, together with digitised images of the original registers.

The registers of other churches are not so easy to access. The National Archives of Scotland hold some original registers from the Episcopal Church, and also some microfilms. Quakers, Methodists, and

Congregationalists were also active in Scotland. Some of their registers are held locally, some have been deposited with the National Archives of Scotland. Some marriage registers can be located in:
*   Scottish Archive Network: Online Catalogue
    www.scan.org.uk/catalogue
    Roman Catholics were persecuted until the mid-eighteenth century, and few registers earlier than 1800 survive. Many of those which do survive have been digitised for the Scotlands People website. The National Archives of Scotland hold copies of some registers. Others have been deposited in the:
*   Scottish Catholic Archive
    www.scottishcatholicarchives.org.uk

The authoritative guide to Scottish registers is:
*   STEEL, D.J., & STEEL, A.A.E. *Sources for Scottish genealogy and family history.* National index of parish registers **12**. Society of Genealogists, 1970.

A number of marriage databases for Scotland are listed in:
*   RAYMOND, STUART A. *Scottish family history on the web: a directory.* 2nd ed. FFHS, 2005.

18. Newspapers
A huge amount of information of relevance to family historians is contained in local newspapers. The *Stamford Mercury,* for example, reported on the cancellation of the banns at Heckington mentioned above (p.12). The intended bridegroom was required to make a public renunciation of any claim to the bride, before his father was able to marry her. The match of Sleighton Nash and Ann Hore attracted such opposition from family members that 'it was found necessary to have two constables to guard the bride and groom to and from church'.

Unusual events are, of course, what sells newspapers. But much more important, in the present context, are the marriage anouncements which were frequently made in personal small advertisements. Unfortunately, few of these are indexed, and at present it is only worth searching them for information if you have a rough idea of the location and the date of the marriage. However, an important digitisation project is currently in progress, and many nineteenth-century newspapers are already searchable online. Visit:
*   British Newspapers 1800-1900.
    http://newspapers.bl.uk/blcs
This project is based on the holdings of the British Library's newspaper collections. Details of these collections, and of a number of other projects based on them, can be found at:

- British Library Newspaper Collections
  www.bl.uk/reshelp/findhelprestype/news/blnewscoll

If your ancestors were prominent people, they may have placed marriage announcements in the *Times*. The *Times index* is widely available in libraries, and also online. The online index can sometimes be accessed free through public library websites:

- Times Online
  archive.timesonline.co.uk/tol/archive

Most local studies libraries have backruns of newspapers covering their own areas. A comprehensive listing of local newspapers, giving locations, and prepared with the family historian in mind, is provided by:

- GIBSON, JEREMY, LANGSTON, BRETT, & SMITH, BRENDA W.
  Local newspapers 1750-1920: England and Wales, Channel Islands, Isle of Man: a select location list. 2nd ed. F.F.H.S., 2002.

19. Divorce

The dissolution of a marriage was not possible in England between the Reformation and 1858, except by Act of Parliament. Nevertheless, a number of alternatives were open to incompatible partners. Desertion was the simplest. The parties sometimes agreed to a private separation, and drew up a deed to separate, which might be enrolled on the Close rolls (now in TNA, C54). The church courts might grant a decree of nullity or annulment. None of these alternatives allowed the possibility of remarriage. For further information, see:

- Divorce Records before 1858
  www.nationalarchives.gov.uk/catalogue/
  RdLeaflet.asp?sLeafletID=260

The Court for Divorce and Matrimonial Causes was established in 1858, with the power to grant divorce. In 1873, it became a part of the Probate, Divorce and Admiralty Division of the Supreme Court of Judicature. Currently, most divorces are granted in county courts. It is possible to obtain certified copies of decrees nisi and absolute for all divorces. Some case files survive in TNA, class J77. These files include some where the divorce petition was unsuccesful. For detailed information about divorce records, visit:

- Divorce Records in England and Wales after 1858
  www.nationalarchives.gov.uk/catalogue/
  RdLeaflet.asp?sLeafletID=53

20. Research Techniques

You are likely to begin your research with a range of information provided by family members. This information should be treated as unproven until you can verify it. It is necessary to obtain birth, marriage and death certificates from the GRO or from local registrars. The information they provide is likely to enable you to check census returns, which are available every ten years between 1841 and 1911. The census will probably give you clues to earlier marriages: young children probably mean that a marriage can be traced a few years previously in the same place. Many other sources may also give you clues that will enable you to trace entries in marriage registers. Wills, monumental inscriptions, name lists, occupational sources, and a variety of other documents all provide useful evidence.

Tracing family history is not just a matter of pressing a few buttons on the internet. There are numerous other sources that are likely to give you valuable information. You will need to visit libraries and record offices to explore them. And you will need to consult a manual which explains what sources are available, where you can find them, and how to use them. A basic introduction is provided by:

• RAYMOND, STUART A. *Introducing family history.* F.F.H.S., 2006.

The most comprehensive manual is:

• HERBER, MARK. *Ancestral trails.* Sutton, 2004.

21. Some Useful Addresses and Internet Gateways

General Register Office
PO Box 2,
Southport, PR8 2JD
www.gro.gov.uk/gro/content

The National Archives
Kew,
Richmond,
Surrey, TW9 4DU
www.nationalarchives.gov.uk

Guildhall Library
Aldermanbury,
London, EC2V 7HH
www.cityoflondon.gov.uk/corporation/LGNL_Services/
Leisure_and_culture/Libraries/City_of_London_libraries/
guildhall_lib.htm

Record repositories are listed at:

- Archon Directory
  www.nationalarchives.gov.uk/archon
  A directory of the resources of local studies libraries is available at:
- Familia: the UK and Ireland's guide to genealogical resources in
  public libraries
  www.familia.org.uk

For family history societies, see

- Federation of Family History Societies Member Societies
  www.ffhs.org.uk/members2/contacting.php

Family History Centers of the LDS are listed by:

- Family Search: Family History Centers
  www.familysearch.org/Eng/library/FHC/frameset_FHC.asp